CONSIDER *the* BIRDS

12

MEDITATIONS TO DISCOVERING YOUR VALUE

KIMBERLY EDMUNDS

Consider the Birds

ISBN: 9798566393940

Table of Contents

Introduction

Value Scripture

"Look at all the birds—do you think they worry about their existence? They don't plant or reap or store up food, yet your heavenly Father provides them each with food. Aren't you much more valuable to your Father than they?"

–Matthew 6:26 TPT

Throughout my teens and young adult years, I had vowed never to have children. I maintained that ideal into adulthood; but somehow, in my early 30s, the maternal instinct came with a vengeance. For nearly five years my husband and I tried to conceive a child. We underwent several unsuccessful procedures, surgeries, and treatments. The absence of positive results made our love life feel like a science fair project, and we didn't win a prize.

After science failed, we began the arduous process of adoption. It is not surprising that so many children are waiting for parents. They share the wait with the parents waiting for children. Between the FBI fingerprinting, creating a dossier of our entire life, home visits—

and hours of parenting classes the adoption process takes time, effort, and money. Eventually, we arrived at the end of the adoption process and I had one last to-do to check off the long list of requirements: make a family scrapbook. After all the intense scrutiny and endless paperwork yet there I sat, on the floor in the middle of our living room, begrudgingly assembling a family scrapbook.

There is an irony in convincing a woman willing to give up her child that I deserved to be a mother. Nevertheless, I scrutinized every photo that I glued to the pages: a wedding picture to show our love and commitment, pictures of us with the children in our family to prove we loved kids, our recent vacation to the Caribbean exhibited our financial wherewithal. Every photo meant to convince and persuade the myriad of judges that would determine if we were fit to have a child. It seemed so unfair. My head and my hands were acting independently as my resentment was being defied by my fingers gluing the pictures of my husband and me to the pages. *What if this woman does not accept us? This could be our last option. If this fails, we will have to live our life without the joy of being parents.*

The thought of failure was overtaken by a more powerful thought, "Consider the birds." The new thought was like someone speaking clearly, with command and authority. The voice was so urgent that I abandoned the scrapbook and immediately went outside and plopped down on my porch and really began to watch the birds as they flew around me. I watched them leap from limb to limb with calm assurance. They landed on the wimpiest limb without care of whether it could hold their weight. They soared in the sky, alone or with other birds. They flew in formation, changing positions from leader to follower. They chirped, they scampered about the ground. They ate food that lay on the ground. They knowingly took flight at the precise second needed to avoid vehicles or the curious observer who got too close.

Over the years, I have learned many valuable lessons from watching birds. I've learned that I have a loving God that will care for me, provide for me and sustain me because I am worth it. He wants me to live freely with the assurance of provision, protection, and unconditional acceptance. He wants me to live with clarity of purpose seeking Him not things. He wants me to know what birds know: it is not what I *do* that makes me valuable, it is that I *am*. I invite you to follow along as we learn from our feathered friends.

Value Lesson

In our country today, everyone is asserting their need to be heard, pleading for the rest of the world to take notice as if to say, "See me, I matter." Pop up movements like "make America great again," "Black Lives Matter," "#MeToo," are the voices of marginalized people demanding, "VALIDATE ME!" "TELL ME I AM VALUABLE!" The truth is that all of these people are right, they do matter. The question is not "Do they matter?", the question is "Why do they matter?" It is not because of their race, gender, socio-economic status or political position. It is not because they are citizens or illegal immigrants. It's not because they have a home in the suburbs or under a bridge; whether they are the CEO or the frontline worker. They matter, we all matter because God created us with intrinsic value. He sealed us with a stamp of approval when He declared "It is very good."

Value Prayer

Father, everything in creation reflects your splendor. Teach me my value as I consider the birds.

Value Practice

Spend time outside. Observe the birds. Note their movements and behaviors. Write down what you discovered or things you could relate to?

Identity

Value Scripture

"Then you will know I AM one with the Father. You will know YOU ARE one with Me and I AM one with you."

–John 14:20 CEV

God created birds with an innate and accurate compass. When they head out for flight, they set their compass for the destination and the duration of the flight. Errors in the flight plan can prove fatal. We see them freely soaring above and we make the mistake of thinking their lives are largely carefree. In fact, their flight path is purposeful, not random. They are largely flying to secure food, warmth, a mate—things that sustain their life and species. During flight, they encounter many environmental circumstances that serve to challenge them as they try to reach their destination.

Amazingly, these incredible creatures draw from what they are to meet every challenge. If they need to migrate to a warmer climate and meet with the headwinds of warmer air, they ensure they travel across lands with cooler temperature that they know will provide the balance of a tailwind. If a driving rain veers them off course, they recalculate the duration of the flight and determine if they have enough fuel to finish the journey. They allow themselves to drift off of the original course to find a place to refuel: an offshore oil rig or a ship where they take a free and restful ride to dry land. Or if a perching place cannot be found, they allow themselves to drift downward toward the sea, to conserve their strength until they reach fairer winds.

Our intelligent and magnificent God, foresaw the life of the bird and designed every detail for them to be birds. And He made us to be humans, made in His own image. He gave us our identity in the design.

Jesus came to provide a profile of what we should be like. How to be like our creator. With conviction He identified Himself:

I am – the bread of life

I am – the light of the world

I am – the door

I am – the true vine

I am – the good shepherd

I am – the resurrection and life

I am – the way the truth and the life

He gave us a profile of who He was and He repeatedly reminded us of the fact that He was the express image of His Father, our creator. Early in His journey, He was affirmed by the Father when God publicly declared, "This is my <u>beloved </u>Son in whom I am <u>well pleased.</u>" It was out of this clear and secure identity that Jesus walked the earth with confidence, purpose, and authority.

Throughout His time on earth, people, often religious people, tried to tell Him what He was <u>not,</u> but Jesus walked confidently in His, *I am.*

Value Lesson

God took the time to carefully design the birds of the air and every living creature. But when He created human beings, He created us in His own image. He gave us His likeness and characteristics, His identity. He placed us in His family and became our Father. This makes us His most valued creation.

Value Prayer

Father, please reveal to me who I am and what it means to be identified as Yours. Show me where I have been the victim of identity theft. Help me to know that You and I are one, just as Jesus prayed. Anchor me in this new identity so that I can know my true value and I can walk with confidence, purpose, and authority in the earth.

Value Practice

Write down the "I AM' statements you would use to describe yourself?

In what ways do you identify with Jesus' "I AM" statements?

What are some of the headwinds (things that take you out of the plan of God)?

What are some of the tailwinds (things that help you to align with God's plan)?

What circumstances in life cause you to drift from God's plan?

How might you set a course that keeps you in God's plan for your life?

Provision

I felt a surge of joy as I pressed the button for the crosswalk light change so that I could walk over to the beach. The walk signal illuminated and I crossed quickly while I checked my cell phone to retrieve the code to the gated entry. The gate clicked locked behind me as I made my way down the creaky wooden ramp. I was delighted to see that no one was on the sandy stretch of beach. The quietness brought an instant stillness to my mind and heart. From the ramp, my eyes soaked in the white sugary sand and the gentle flow of the ocean as it made its way to the shore, wave after wave.

I had planned to simply sit on the benches that lined the ramp but the calmness of the waves and the sand drew me in closer. The sand was dry and cool. There was an ocean breeze that provided just enough relief from the sun overhead. The sand squished between my toes and I felt refreshed.

My eyes became fixed on the sandpipers that were gathering on the shore. They scampered about hurriedly as if they were late to an important appointment. They moved from spot to spot rapidly poking their beak into the sand to retrieve tasty bugs and worms. Scamper, scamper, poke…scamper, scamper poke. They never seemed disappointed or discouraged as they moved from place to place. There was no doubt that they would find some unsuspecting insect among the seaweed that had been washed ashore by the waves. "Let the waves do the work; we birds can just feast."

I followed the sandpipers as they scampered about, seeking, poking…as if to show me that there is always provision of the things that preserve our lives. In fact, Jesus encouraged us to take no thought to food and clothing because our Father in heaven knows we have need of these things and He will provide if we seek Him first.

As a person that has been passionate about serving the poor, I struggle with the promise of food and shelter that Jesus promised. The fact of the matter is that millions of children die every year from curable diseases because they are poor. And while the number of people living in extreme poverty has decreased over 80% (2 billion people) since 1980, we are far from a world where every human being has food, clothing, and shelter.

The Democratic Republic of Congo (DRC) has the unenviable position of being the poorest country in the world, yet it has an abundant supply of natural resources. Such is the case with many of the poorest countries in the world. War, corruption, unrighteous leadership, and unfair practices of developed countries often prevents many of these places from rising from the bondage of poverty.

Watching the sandpipers as they scampered about finding food to eat, the facts of poverty made me question the Provider of Matthew 6:33. Were the poor children in the third world hungry because they were not seeking first a kingdom of God? The answer came back a resounding NO! The poor children in the third world were hungry because those with the ability to do something about it were not seeking first the kingdom of God. It is up to us to scamper about the earth doing our part to provide for those that cannot provide for themselves. We must poke to find injustices and eliminate it along the stretch of sand God assigns to us.

Value Lesson

As a person of value, it is my responsibility to contribute to others and to give of myself. Because I am valuable I have what I need and more, which makes me able to meet the needs of others. When I meet the needs of others, I become valuable to them, and I bring God glory.

Value Prayer

Father, help me to seek with the confidence of knowing the provision is there, though it be hidden from my immediate sight, you value me too much to let me go without what I need to live abundantly. And as I live abundantly teach me to be a cheerful giver to others, as I do my part in delivering your promise to provide food, clothing, and shelter.

Value Practice

Think of someone that lacks an essential to life (clothing, food, shelter). Write down the ways that you might personally meet their need.

Purpose

Value Scripture

"Aren't two sparrows sold for a penny? Yet not one of them falls to the ground without your Father's consent. But even the hairs of your head have all been counted. So, don't be afraid therefore; you are worth more than many sparrows."

–Matthew 10:29-31 HCSB

Birds have skills to navigate the most powerful of storms. Tracking systems placed on migratory birds show that they have an amazing ability to correct course and to use hurricane force winds to propel them to safe ground. One whimbrel was tracked entering Hurricane Sandy at 7 mph and came out the other side at 90 mph to safety. They ride out the storm, fill up with nourishment, and then they fly home.

When hurricanes come, amazingly, there are no bird corpses strewn along the sidewalks and yards. Some of them find themselves on top of the mountains of foreign lands providing local bird watchers a rare view. Navigation skills like the whimbrels' is what my friend Kaye needed. Like the birds, she did not want to become a victim of her storm. But in that moment, her life was in a whirlwind. Everything she had known was in chaos. After 25 years of working at the same hospital, she was being transferred to a new location, presumably so that they could set her up to be fired. She tried to remain composed as tears welled up in her eyes, some of them escaping as she tried to control her emotions. I adjusted my chair so that I could get closer to her, anticipating that she might need the hug of a friend. Placing my hand on her shoulder released her to fall into my arms; I could feel the disappointment and confusion that consumed her heart.

After a beautifully spotless career, she was falsely accused of mistreating one of her employees. Her boss thought it would be best to move Kaye to a new location until things "blew over." As a hospice nurse, she could not imagine leaving her precious patients; they were like family. They had taught her so much about gratitude, endurance and priorities. Despite her insistence that the decision was unfair, within one week she found herself 20 miles from her former patients and the families that had come to trust her with their dying loved one. All seemed lost, her career, her families, her life.

A few weeks after that tearful meeting in her kitchen, I ran into Kaye. She raced excited toward me. There was so much for us to catch up on. She was elated as she told the stories of each new patient, and her new co-workers. There is Miss Sally who loves Jesus and just wants to get on to heaven but the medicines keep making her better. Miss Sally was furious that she made it to the New Year, how dare God. When Kaye came in to wish her Happy New Year, she responded "What's good about it?" "You're what's good about it, Miss Sally." Kaye's response brought a reluctant smile to Miss Sally's face. And there was Mr. Leo whose daughter, Ashley was really having a hard time watching him die. In true form, Kaye was able to show her the value of those final moments encouraging her to write down all of the ways she would miss Mr. Leo. She encouraged Ashley to read her "I'll miss you" notes to Mr. Leo on her visits. Ashley enjoyed those final moments and so did Mr. Leo. "You made these last days so special, Kaye" was the first line of the thank you note that Ashley left at the nurse's station.

Blown off course, Kaye embraced the wind. Things felt out of her control, but when she settled down she saw the new scenery and learned to love her new home. Admittedly, she would not wish this storm on her enemies, but she would not trade the flight path for anything in the world because without it she would not have met Miss Sally, Mr. Leo, and her dear Ashley. I saw a new Kaye that day, full of purpose and contentment realizing that she had landed in the right place, at the right time.

Value Lesson

We are valuable to God. No circumstance, opinion, or event can add to or take away from our value. At times, God needs us to see this truth from a different "mountain," giving others and us a different perspective. Regardless of the situation we are in, we live under His protection, His provision, and His purpose. And we carry our value and worth with us to each destination.

Value Prayer

Father, I know that you still command the wind and the sea. This situation in my life is devastating to me. I am scared and bitter and lost. Help me to get to a place of safety so that I might catch my breath. In this new normal, open my eyes to those who have eyes on me and help me to bring you glory even though I am tattered and hurt. In the whirlwind, help me see that my suffering does not mean I am undeserving of your peace. Let me be encouraged in knowing that nothing can separate me from your love or the value you place on my life.

Value Practice

If you are currently in a storm, list the people and places around you. If you are not in a storm, then did you survive? How? After the storm, who and what did you see? Did you embrace your new normal or did you make your way back to the old life?

Pre-Packaged

Value Scripture

"Everything is possible to the one who believes."

–Mark 9:23 HCSB

It's always funny when I commute to work and, somewhere along the journey, I ask myself how I got there. The routine of driving the same route numbs us to our familiar surroundings. First, the highway, jammed with cars, trucks, exhaust and road rage. Then the exit, causing cars to come to a screeching halt as the eight lanes narrow to one. Inevitably, a driver peers pitifully over to me hoping I will let them cut the line. I decide whether or not to be generous and let them in. There is a surge of unfounded power when I do. Without a real awareness of my journey, as I pull into my driveway, I begin to press the garage door button hooked to the sun visor.

I was met with pants, shirts, and shoes hanging like stiff zombies from the garage ceiling. It became apparent that my husband was overpreparing us for our first visit to the third world, an opportunity to meet the children in a school that we helped build.

My husband had sprayed repellent over every inch of our clothing to prevent mosquitoes from biting through the fabric and depositing malaria into our skin. When I entered the house, I was greeted with all of the other trappings of a well-planned trip to the third world: iPod, books, SOS card, cliff bars, cipro, malaria pills and more bug repellent to apply directly to our skin.

The distance from my home to Ghana is a little over twice the distance that the golden plover takes to commute between its two homes of Hawaii and Alaska. This bird lives in Alaska in the summer and makes an annual trip to Hawaii for the winter, almost 2500 miles one-way. The plover does not swim, which precludes stopovers or lunch breaks since the entire trip is over water. We, on the other hand, make the annual mission to Accra aboard a well-crafted, well-attended plane. Yet, the golden plover takes his voyage without thought or preparation, it knows it must go and it goes instinctively.

We prepare for every detail and every possible circumstance; we create our plan Bs and rainy-day holdbacks. We often focus on failure versus destiny. It's not to suggest that we don't plan or set a course for our lives. It is necessary that we set goals and make wise decisions. Even birds calculate the duration and flight path before taking off to their destination. But they trust their "packaging" and they go. They remember the former journey and that there might be obstacles, but they go knowing they can handle what comes their way. They go, assuming the flight will be successful.

Value Lesson

Like the birds, I have what I need for the journey. Because God knows the plan He has for me, He pre-programmed and packaged me for success. I fly above the expanse of my fears and doubt.

Value Prayer

Father, even though I am entering unfamiliar territory I know that you are with me. I'm trying my best to prepare for what is to come but I am anxious and uncertain of what will happen. Help me to remember that you have a plan for my life and that you pre-packaged me for success. Help me to believe that I have what it takes to fulfill the plans you have for me.

Value Practice

Think of a situation or endeavor that you feel you should be tackling but have not launched because of fear or self-doubt. Do you believe God gave you the gifts, talents and abilities to be successful? What if you knew you would not fail, what would you do today?

Peace

Value Scripture

"You are my hiding place; You protect me from trouble. You surround me with joyful shouts of deliverance."

–Psalm 32:7 HCSB

In today's environment of climate change, we are told that we will have more severe weather. Regardless as to your political leanings, you can't go anywhere without people commenting on history making weather conditions. The recent Hurricane Dorian devastated the Abacos Islands with its 185 mph winds leaving families and homes shattered. Experts tell us that hurricanes are made up of three main parts: the eye, the eye wall, and the rain bands. The eye wall and the rain bands create the most destruction.

The eye is warm, calm, with light winds of less than 15 mph. Like Hurricane Dorian, Matthew was a category 5 hurricane, yet seagulls were spotted inside of the eye. They apparently entered in through the end of the spiraling wind and made their way to the eye, where they hung out until the storm subsided, or they traveled with it to the shore. Despite the chaotic destructive force of hurricane winds, birds find a way to survive.

My personal hurricane came at the age of 19. I was married too young to the wrong guy and my life was plunged into a downward spiral of emotional abuse. There were many days when I thought I would never make it out of the marriage alive. There were so many forces against me: the constant barrage of regrets that I had: not listening to my parents' wise advice, my Christian beliefs that marriage was for better or worse, until death, my abusive husband who convinced me that it was all my fault for making him angry.

My confusion bombarded me like literal rain bands, relentless and powerful. My thoughts were stronger than my faith, and hope could not survive. Sitting on my bed one night, I was overtaken with hopelessness and began to sob. Somehow through the torrential tears, I caught sight of a lifeline, an 800# that flashed across the bottom of the TV screen. I found myself doing what I had scoffed at so many times before; I dialed the prayer line. The young lady on the line sounded young and inexperienced, too much like me. But at this point, she was all I had, so I shared my situation. Within a few minutes she said nine words that changed the course of my life: "God wants us to do what makes for peace."

Peace. It was what I longed for. That young lady lit a pathway directly to the peaceful eye of the hurricane—God wanted me to have peace and protection, not turmoil and fear. The unhealthy relationship had taken me away from His ultimate purpose, but there was a way back, I just had to hang out in His peace until I could travel with the winds to a safe shore. In my case, that travel did not come unchallenged. There were many times that I wanted to just stay in the comfort of that young ladies' words. But eventually, I jumped into the subsiding winds and found my way back to my parents' house. It was scary at first but I eventually regained my sense of worth and continued along my journey.

Sometimes life comes at us like a hurricane—the untimely death of a spouse, a child that has strayed into drug addiction, a job loss, financial ruin, a failed marriage—we have to learn to do what birds do: find the eye of the storm and then, ultimately, back home.

Value Lesson

There is often loss of life and property in strong storms. God knows I am too valuable to remain in turmoil and devastation. As I trust and acknowledge Him instead of leaning on my own understanding of the situation, He will give me a path to peace.

Value Prayer

Lord, I feel like I just got hit by hurricane-force winds. Everything around me seems destroyed and unfixable. My very foundation has been uprooted and I see devastation all around me. I'm hitting an enormous wall of pain and hurt and I can't see my way out. My mind, body and soul are spinning out of control. It's too much for me. Help me find the peaceful center until it passes over.

Value Practice

Think of a time when a life situation came at you with such force. Even though there were warnings, you could not get out of the way. What was the situation? When did you find the eye? How did you navigate the wind?

Perspective

Value Scripture

"Now we see things imperfectly, like puzzling reflections in a mirror, but then we will see everything with perfect clarity."

–1 Corinthians 13:12 NLT

"All of these birds seem different. I bet there are at least 20 different types of birds at this beach," my husband declared. His statement piqued my interest as we sat waiting for the splendor of another sunset at Bidawee Beach. "No there are not that many different birds, the majority of these birds are pelicans," I rebutted. I knew my comment would spark a fun debate because my husband can never resist proving me wrong when I state my opinion as fact.

"Pelicans fly high above the sea, and these birds are flying at high speed just inches above the water and then use their beaks to nab a fish," he insisted. In the middle of the banter, a large black and white bird with a bright orange beak comes into view. This bird was flying fast, close to the surface of the water. I also began to notice the curious little birds that scurried along the beach, noodling with their beaks into the sand. They would often stop and stare with their black marble eyes as if contemplating where to poke next.

The truth of the matter is that there are skimmers, pelicans, and sandpipers and a multitude of other birds that make the shoreline their home. Each bird species has their own way of living on the earth, and they function freely in their perfect design.

Skimmers are designed with a beak that is long on the bottom and short on the top. When they forage for food, they place the longer portion just below the surface of the water in order to feel the fish; then they open the top portion of the beak and scoop the unsuspecting fish out of the water and into their mouth. The pelican, with its sharp vision, can spot fish from the air and then they plunge in and snag it. The sandpiper probes the ground seeking out insects and other small invertebrates. Whether skimming, plunging, or probing birds are using every part of their design to eat. They do so knowing that there is provision; it's all in the feeling, the seeing, and the seeking until they eat. It doesn't matter if they have to do so from flight, ground, or water.

Value Lesson

God has provided everything we need to live abundantly but it is not always in plain view. Sometimes, like the skimmer, we have to come in close. Sometimes, like the pelican, we have to pull up a little higher and see things from a different point of view; perhaps embrace a reality different than the one we are comfortable with. Sometimes, like the sandpiper, we have to probe in various places, often coming up short but being willing to keep on trying and seeking until we come upon what we need.

Value Prayer

Father, I know that You promised to always provide for me. Right now, I feel empty and unsatisfied. It feels as if I am ungrateful for all that you give me, so help me to do better. Give me the right perspective so that I can find what you have for me. If I need to see better, sharpen my vision and discernment. If I am trying to avoid my true feelings, help me to open myself up to you so that you can heal my broken places. If I'm not asking enough questions or if I stopped seeking too soon, renew my curiosity for truth and my energy to keep going.

Value Practice

Think of a situation where you are still longing for more or a prayer that you feel has not been answered. What is the status of the situation from your perspective today? Interview three people you trust and get their perspective on your situation. What did you discover?

Protection

Value Scripture

"He will cover you with His wings; You will be safe in His care; His faithfulness will protect and defend you."

–Psalm 91:4 GNB

Walking out of my front door one day, I was immediately attacked by an angry bird. Unaware of the nest that she had built just inside the gable, I attempted to leave for work, and again this swallow swooped in with her wings flapping, and high-pitched chirping. I closed the door and decided to exit from the garage. For several days my husband and I watched the mother swallow perched on the neighbor's roof across the street. As soon as we attempted to open the door she would race in like the Angry Birds in the video game, chirping, flapping her wings, fiercely protecting her vulnerable babies. She was so protective that I named her Baby Mama Swallow.

Daily, my husband threatened to take a broom to the nest, lamenting that Baby Mama Swallow had usurped his authority as owner of the house while not contributing to the mortgage payment. My pleading and compassion prevailed to give Baby Mama Swallow a few more days to nurture her babies from the nest. Eventually nature ran its course and the baby birds became mature enough to fly. Needless to say, the abandoned nest made its way into the trash receptacle so as to prevent any future birds from taking up residence at our home.

There are times during our life's journey when we are babies too. We find ourselves in situations where we have no experience and no tools to survive or thrive. Vulnerable to the "broom" and living in a fragile state. Perhaps we are newly divorced and living on our own for the first time. Or we are a teen mom who does not know how to raise a child; or we open up a business that has the potential to fall flat on its face.

Just like His eye is on the sparrow, His eyes are on us.

Value Lesson

I am valuable and therefore I am protected. When I am vulnerable, my Protector will come, wings flapping, chirping loudly to shield me. When it seems He is no longer coming to my rescue, it means I'm ready to fly on my own.

Value Prayer

Father, I feel so inadequate for the task ahead of me. I'm in a situation that I don't feel that I am ready for. I don't have the skills. I don't have the money, the re-sources to be successful so I'm scared. Help me see what you see in me. And as I struggle through this place, let me feel your covering and your protective presence.

Value Practice

Consider a situation where you felt totally vulnerable. What was the situation? How did you overcome your fear? What if you knew for sure that God was watching the situation? What if you knew for sure He placed you there? What would be different?

Connected

Value Scripture

"A person standing alone can be attached and defeated, but two can stand back to back and conquer. Three are even better, for a triple braided cord is not easily broken."

–Ecclesiastes 4:12 NLT

It's always a pleasure to drive to the beach with my husband. The more times we take the five-hour trip it seems the distance becomes shorter. Usually, I am engrossed in a conference call or sorting through email on my iPhone. My husband is sorting through music or listening to sports talk radio. We have taken the route so often we make the trip without GPS, or Google Maps—we know every turn, every landmark, and every annoying variation of speed as we enter the small towns. We can smell the ocean as we get closer to the coast. The road seems to be as familiar with us as we are with it.

We reached the beach just as the sun was setting. We walked hurriedly as not to miss the spectacular canvas God was about to paint as the sun cast its final light on the sky. Just as we reached the beach ramp, I was re-freshed by the breeze as it rushed over my face. In the distance I could hear the giggles from children romp-ing in the ocean waves.

Pelicans were flying in unison over our heads. They ap-peared to be stacked one above the other in a hierar-chy of flight, but on closer look they were in a single horizontal line. Flap Flap Flap Soar. Each bird follows a certain rhythm. Flap Flap Flap Soar. Each in turn, per-fect timing. They fly as one, no bird taking on too much of the burden of flapping or too much of the soaring.

In the distance the big fiery ball of light peacefully dropped from my sight. I imagine it gratefully sinking into the cool ocean waters after a long day's work… aah!. Somewhere, on the other side of the world, peo-ple are waking up, some are driving in rush hour traffic with a view of the sunset from their windshields as it settles over the Pacific Ocean. I feel wondrously con-nected.

Value Lesson

When I know my value, I come to appreciate the value of others. I have much to contribute and when I come into community with others we can soar together, nei-ther of us feeling unimportant or overburdened.

Value Prayer

Lord, help me to know that I am not equipped to do life alone. Show me the community that you have placed around me. Help me to value them and to embrace them. Show me where I fit, so that I can get into the rhythm and flow of your Spirit. I want to be effective for the kingdom and I cannot go it alone.

Value Practice

Think of a situation that you are trying to tackle on your own without success. Who in your community could help you if you asked?

Voices

Value Scripture

"The Lord God has given me a tongue of those who are instructed to know how to sustain the weary with a word. He awakens me each morning. He awakens my ear to listen like those being instructed."

–Isaiah 50:4 HCSB

A morning walk in my neighborhood can be quite refreshing and insightful. I've learned to walk without my iPod so that I can take in my surroundings. I become aware of mundane things like the slight angle of the sidewalk pitched in such a way as to prevent water from pooling, the variations of my neighbors' lawns—some so meticulously groomed they could be mistaken for the Augusta National golf course. Others nicely mowed and edged but more brown than green. Sprinklers pop up and startle my thoughts but provide a much-needed coolness to the air at the right time when my breathing labors uphill.

But what I enjoy the most is the sound of the chirping, winnowing, rattling birds. No matter what time of day I'm walking, the birds provide a familiar chorus.

I've learned that what sounds like singing to the human ear is really communication between birds. I call it Bird Tweets. Bird Tweets have a carefully scripted purpose. At times, it is the mating call of the males determined to perpetuate the species for years to come, or the repetitive song of a mother protecting her territory from invasion. Birds sing in flight, each note like breadcrumbs left so that others can follow their path. They sing with high-pitched tweets to warn other birds that a predator is near or to rejoice when food is found. They learn complicated melodies while nesting over their babies. They sing as if they have sheets of music mounted on an easel. Each tweet is distinct and important. Birds know what sound to respond to.

Like the various "voices" of the birds, we too have voices. There is the voice of the world limiting us by our stature and position in life. There is our own voice, the internal critic that rates us 1 to 5 on each success and failure. We hear these voices and we respond, often without evaluation.

We assume that the voice that tells us we should chase the approval of others is as valid as the voice that tells us we are fearfully and wonderfully made. Like the birds, we need to know what voices to respond to.

We must learn the voice of God…. still, quiet, powerful. The voice of all that is Good, the voice of the one we should walk with, believe, and trust.

Value Lesson

Jesus said that His followers know His voice. He was confident that we would not follow the voice of those who mean us harm. God's voice has a certain tone and pitch. I need to hear His call to communion, prayer, obedience and mission. The voice that leads to provision, protection, and purpose. The voice that tells us we are "much more valuable than they."

Value Prayer

Lord, teach me to hear and know your voice. I want to recognize the tone, tenor, and cadence of your voice. And then, Lord, let me give me my voice. A voice that has the sound waves that mimic You. When I speak, let the sound be healing, and comforting to the listener. Words that encourage and uplift. Words that create life.

Value Practice

Ask God to begin to speak to you upon awakening each morning for the next seven days. Place a journal beside your bed and record the first thought you hear when you wake up each day.

Order

Value Scripture

"A fierce windstorm arose, and the waves were break-
ing over the boat, so that the boat was already being
swamped. But He was in the stern sleeping on the
cushion. So, they woke Him up and said to Him,
'Teacher! Don't you care that we're going to die?' He
got up, rebuked the wind and said to the sea, 'Si-
lence! Be still!' The wind ceased, and there was a
great calm. Then He said to them, 'why are you fear-
ful? Do you still have no faith?'"

–Mark 4: 37-40 HCSB

"Our son killed himself! Please come!"

From the moment we received the frantic call from our
dear friends, the tragic sequence of events began to
unfold like the frantic birds that greeted us when we
arrived in Kansas from Atlanta. How does anyone get
to a place of complete hopelessness where ending life
becomes a viable solution? Yet every two minutes in
America, someone ends their life. This statistic took on
human form and stared us in the face, up close, too
close.

We quickly picked up our rental car and headed to the hotel. The temperature in the car registered 19 degrees as we drove along Hwy 54. The day was cold and gray as if to align to the somber occasion that caused us to return to Kansas. I looked up and saw a flock of birds flying, frantically in different directions. Just when I thought there would be a feathered collision in the sky, they suddenly made an orderly landing on the top of a billboard; they lined up like soldiers called to attention by their sergeant, all facing one direction, calm, peaceful and confident.

Upon arrival at our hotel, we called our friends to meet us in the lobby; they looked as if all the life had drained from their bodies. I saw confusion in their eyes, and as we embraced them they collapsed in our arms exhausted by sorrow. We stood silently in the lobby with these two friends in our arms, knowing that no words would satisfy. We slowly made our way to the small table and chairs where they began to recount the horrific events that led them to this point of grief and loss. We sat together with intermittent times of inconsolable sadness and distractions of laughter as they thought of happier memories of their son.

Like frantic, colliding birds, life can become a mass of confusion in an instant: A sudden fatal car accident, loss of a job, divorce, discovery of infidelity. All that we know can be dismantled and shaken to the core. But, like the wildly-flying birds quickly formed into an orderly landing on the narrow edge of billboards, God can quickly restore order to our chaotic situation. He gives us the strength to make sense out of our pain.

Value Lesson

God values me too much to allow me to remain in chaos and turmoil. In time, the shattered pieces of my life will line up so that I can prepare to move closer to my purpose.

Value Prayer

Dear Father, when everything around me turns to chaos, when I can't see my way and don't know where to turn, when my mind is full of turmoil and confusion, please come and restore order. Hover over me like you did when you created this earth, bringing light to darkness, providing a clear, well-lit path for my feet. I'll hope confidently in You, as you prepare me for my new normal.

Value Practice

See yourself on a boat when a storm comes up. Feel the wind and see the lightning. Feel the churn of your stomach. Notice your thoughts as you think of your family, the fear.

Chicken Little

Value Scripture

"Jerusalem, Jerusalem! Your people have killed the prophets and have stoned the messengers who were sent to you. I have often wanted to gather your people as a hen gathers her chicks under her wings but you wouldn't let me."

Matthew 23:37 CEV

The Bible describes God as a nurturer. He is the One who "hovers" like a bird over the chaotic earth in Genesis; one of His Hebrew names is El Shaddai, which literally means the mighty breasted one, like the mighty feathery breast of an eagle. And then Jesus lamenting that He often wanted to gather His people like a hen gathers her babies.

A picture is worth a thousand words and I watched the TV screen with amazement as a hen gathered her brood of chicks in the woods. She was vigilant as she encouraged each chick to stay close. The curve of her neck darted in all directions; her round black eyes viewed her surroundings with steely determination to "not lose one." With her legs tucked, her lofty wings expanded her body and she settled down.

Each chick instinctively nudged their way through the layers of her feathers until no part of their furry bodies could be seen. To someone observing the settled hen, having not seen the journey, this looked like a hen plunked down to rest in the woods.

There are times when we need to nudge our way under the Father's wings and find comfort and protection. He wants to gather us but we must be willing…willing to say we are vulnerable, willing to admit that we need more maturity, willing to stay in the incubator of His word and prophetic voice until it is our time and place to be the gatherer and protector of others.

Value Lesson

When we find ourselves exposed, living without protection or cover, seemingly out of nowhere our Protector will come, wings flapping with power and strength. He has been watching from a distance, determined that we be given the time to fly. He knows the value of us reaching maturity.

Value Prayer

Dear God, I repent of pride and self-willed determination. I confess that I have "killed" the advice and warnings of those in my life that tried to bring me Your word and command. Give me a humble heart and a willing spirit that allows you to gather me under your wings until it is safe for me to move into my destiny. While I rest under your wings, I feel the value you have for me, help me grow past my vulnerability.

Value Practice

Think about a time when you felt as though you were susceptible to being harmed or attacked. Did you feel comforted or afraid? What did you do to find shelter/protection?

Take a moment to visualize yourself as one of the baby chicks in the story nestled under the hen.

Tenacity

Value Scripture

"The soul of the sluggard craves and gets nothing,
while the soul of the diligent is richly supplied."

–Proverbs 13:4 ESV

It was a cool sunny day out by the restaurant pond. I agreed to meet a colleague for dinner. The temperature was pleasant during this time of year, but I knew it would not be long before the heat and humidity descended on us once the final days of spring gave way to summer, so we decided to take advantage of the pleasant weather rather than eat inside. My colleague commented on how well I had done in my new job despite his initial concerns.

Our conversation was interrupted when one of the ducks from the pond waddled up to us with curious and demanding eyes. My friend opined how the ducks had been overfed by the restaurants customers and were now too fat to fly south, so they just hung around the pond year-round hoping that someone would feed them. Decidedly, Waddles could lose a few pounds. He was created with the ability to forage for food, but the restaurant patrons conditioned him to expect that food came without work.

"Consider the birds, they neither sow, reap, or gather." We hear these words and we envy the easy carefree life of the bird. We watch them playfully scamper about the stretches of sand along the shore and in the next minute they take flight effortlessly. The truth is that bird life is difficult. They fly not out of a sense of adventure, they fly because they must: to escape the cold northern weather, to find food, to secure a mate, to avoid a predator. Birds instinctively know they must survive and that means flight and food constantly.

Waddles found a luxury refuge alongside the restaurant retention pond. He did not question the provision, he simply embraced it as part of living.

Value Lesson

I am too valuable to succumb to ease and comfort. When I don't do what I was made to do, I become dependent on people who might not have my best interest at heart. But I need not make life too difficult or overcomplicated; when things come with ease, I accept it as God's favor.

Value Prayer

Lord, I don't want to take short cuts or take the easy way out. Help me to see the lesson in pushing through difficult situations. Whether it's learning something new or a painful situation, let me remember that there is victory on the other side of pain. I don't want to live a life of ease that does not help me to be my best self.

Value Practice

Think of a difficult situation where you took the easy way out. What did you learn or discover? What would have been the outcome if you had worked through the difficulty?

Acknowledgements

I want to thank my husband Keith for his undying support and encouragement on the journey of completing this devotional. You always believed in me, even when I doubted myself. You are always my hero.

I thank my Lord and Savior Jesus Christ. Since You came into my life over 40 years ago, my life has never been the same. You spoke loudly to me to consider the birds. And as I sat on my front porch that fateful day, You began to show me just how much You value my life. Without You I am nothing. Thank You for helping me to let go of my fears and release these words that You gave me. I am forever Yours.

About the Author

Kimberly Edmunds is first and foremost a Jesus follower. She worked in various executive positions in the telecommunications industry before retiring to build a customer and employee experience consultancy, SadlerAllen. SadlerAllen donates over 60% of its profits to help vulnerable children in Africa and Haiti through her family foundation, HopeFeathers.

She earned an economics degree from the University of Southern California and lives in Florida with her husband Keith.